# The Russian War

# The Russian War: 1941-1945

EDITED BY DANIELA MRAZKOVA AND VLADIMIR REMES

INTRODUCTION BY HARRISON SALISBURY

PREFACE AND NOTES BY A. J. P. TAYLOR

E. P. DUTTON | NEW YORK

First American edition 1977 published by E. P. Dutton,
a division of Sequoia-Elsevier
Publishing Company, Inc., New York

*Library of Congress Cataloging in Publication Data*
Main entry under title: The Russian war, 1941-1945.
Translation of Fotografovali válku.
1. World War, 1939-1945—Campaigns—Russia—Pictorial works.
2. Russia—History—German occupation, 1941-1944—Pictorial works.
3. News photographers. I. Mrázková, Daniela. II. Remeš, Vladimír.
D764.F6813   1977      940.54'21      77-1970
ISBN: 0-525-19560-2
Published simultaneously in Canada by Clarke, Irwin & Company
Limited, Toronto and Vancouver

Designed by Ann Gold

10 9 8 7 6 5 4 3 2 1

First Edition

# Contents

# Preface: A People at War

A. J. P. TAYLOR

In World War II the camera came of age as an instrument of information and propaganda. Cameramen recorded the German offensive in France and the pathetic columns of refugees. They recorded the Japanese attack on Pearl Harbor and the sinking of *The Prince of Wales*. They recorded the battle of El Alamein and the landings on D-day. They also showed life on the home front: the effects of bombing, the queues, the workers in the factories. There have been innumerable illustrated books on the war and its various aspects. I myself wrote one of them and of course looked at many more photographs than I used. I have helped the writers of other illustrated histories. I imagined that I had gotten beyond surprise and knew all the visual aspects of World War II.

I was wrong. The collection of Soviet photographs that this book presents has stunned and inspired me. It has no parallel. This is not a record of war from on high as seen by the commanders of the time and by historians later. It is the record of a people at war and of their experiences.

Because many events of the Russian War are unfamiliar to Western readers, I have provided a brief introduction (set in italics) to each of the episodes from Moscow to Berlin.

# Introduction

HARRISON SALISBURY

There is no more dangerous art than that of war photography. It is no accident that of 30 war correspondents killed in Vietnam half were photographers—American, Vietnamese, Japanese, French, English.

In World War II the story was the same, and, with the possible exception of the war in the Pacific, no theater of hostilities was more perilous than the Eastern Front—the ever-shifting line of engagement where the Soviet Red Army first retreated along a 1,200-mile front, then stood, fought and finally destroyed Hitler's armies.

To most Americans the details of the Nazi-Soviet hostilities are almost unknown. Yet the war in the East became a human hell of indescribable dimensions: the 900-day siege of Leningrad, in which more than 1,300,000 persons lost their lives; Stalingrad, where Hitler sacrificed a force of 600,000 men; Kiev, a fatal trap for 1,500,000 Russians; Kursk-Orel, the world's greatest armored battle, engaging possibly 8,000 tanks and armored vehicles.

In the East the Germans exterminated millions of Jews in the terrible death camps and captured and enslaved possibly 20 million Russians, working and starving them to death. Here great modern cities were laid waste as thoroughly as if by the Hiroshima bomb, and here Russian troops finally brought Adolf Hitler to Götterdämmerung with the storming of Berlin, the Reichstag and the famous bunker where the Nazi leader and some of his henchmen took their own lives.

Almost every step, every act, every tragedy, every defeat, every victory in this calvary of the years 1941–1945 was recorded by the lenses of an incredibly brave, numerous and ingenious band of Soviet photographers. These pictures are among the finest of the war—and the least known in the West.

Soviet editors often speak of Soviet war photography as if the art of the documentary had been invented by the Russians. They point out that even before the Revolution, Russian photographers in the Russo-Japanese War and World War I did outstanding work. This is quite true but somewhat misleading. The role of American photographers, beginning with Brady in the Civil War, is at least as good, and the contribution of German photographers has been impressive.

However, the special phenomenon of Russian photographers in World War II is their remarkable closeness to the field of action. In fact, they are usually *part of* the field of action. This is particularly true of the unequaled combat photographs of the Stalingrad battle

1

from the cameras of Georgi Zelma, Yakov Ryumkin, Georgi Lipskerov and Viktor Tyomin. Stalingrad was a battle fought street by street, building by building, floor by floor, room by room and often man to man. The Soviet cameramen literally shot over the shoulders of combat soldiers and not infrequently alternated between lens and pistol.

Technically all Soviet war photographers had combat status and many played a valiant role in defending the positions from which they focused their cameras. It is sometimes said that the Soviet collections of battle pictures are weak for the early part of the war because the photographers were too busy fighting to use their cameras. It is true that fewer dramatic and significant photos were released in the early stages of the war, but this is not because Soviet cameramen did not take them. Here the fault lies with the Soviet propaganda apparatus, which did not wish at a moment when the country was fighting for its existence to depress morale by distributing dramatic photographs of death and devastation.

The most powerful photographs in this collection equal any ever taken on a battle scene. This is particularly true of those taken by Lipskerov and Zelma at Stalingrad and of Boris Kudoyarov's pictures of the 900-day siege of Leningrad. Kudoyarov spent the whole period of the blockade in Leningrad, the only reporter or photographer to endure the entire siege. He was there in the terrible days when the ration was cut to 100 grams of bread and thousands died each day of starvation, disease and cold. And he was there when the siege was finally lifted in January, 1944. His photographs transmit to us better than words the image of the deadly citadel of ice and cold which Leningrad became during the terrible winter of 1941–42. The May, 1945, end-of-the-war pictures of Berlin are classics. They capture the full flavor of the battered Nazi capital and the almost childlike exuberance of the conquering Russians.

Photographically, the Russians are rightly proud of the quality of their work, proud that it was taken almost entirely with 35-mm. Leicas, proud that the combat photographers shot on the run, thus conveying through their pictures the feeling of movement, accidental drama and raw action.

Many pictures are designed to inspire bravery, confidence, self-sacrifice and resolution—certainly objectives that marked at least some American war photography during World War II. However, in the Korean war and the Vietnam war, under the brilliant influence of David Douglas Duncan, American war photographers became notably more realistic, not flinching from the grime and ugliness of battle as did photographers during World War II.

Probably the most famous picture in this collection, at least in the Soviet Union, is Yevgeni Khaldei's picture of a Red Army soldier waving the Soviet banner over the fallen Reichstag in Berlin in May, 1945. This is the Russian equivalent of the American World War II photograph of the Marines raising the American flag over Iwo Jima.

A photograph reproduced in the Soviet Union during World War II was Max Alpert's picture of Commissar Yeryomenko leading his regiment into action, automatic raised in one hand and the other extended as if to hurl a grenade. It was published and republished in *Pravda* and other Soviet newspapers, used as a poster design and became a kind of symbol of the defiant Red Army. It is a striking composition and in feeling bears close resemblance to Robert Capa's famous picture of the soldier with outstretched arms, shot on the battlefield of the Spanish Civil War.

Despite the skill of the photographers some aspects of the war on the Eastern Front remained beyond their grasp. Alexander Ustinov's portfolio of photographs of the Battle of Moscow in the autumn of 1941, which turned the tide against Hitler and inflicted the first defeat the Nazi armies were to suffer, are as graphic as any in the collection. But even these stirring photographs cannot reflect the full drama of the moment, especially the incredible suffering of the Russian civilians who gave their lives preparing for Moscow's defenses.

Most of the men and women who took these photographs were in their twenties during World War II. Most of them had had little prior experience in any important photography. Most of them won their spurs in battle, and a surprisingly high percentage are still at work professionally.

Each photographer represented in this collection survived the war. Curiously, no pictures by any of the dozens of Soviet photographers killed in the war are included. Thus, we have none of Mikhail Kalashnikov's work taken before his death in the siege of Sevastopol, nor any examples of the work of such men as Sergei

Stunnikov and Mikhail Bernshtein of *Pravda*, Vladimir Ivanov of TASS and the many comrades who died with them at the front.

No collection of Soviet war photography could encompass all of the good work that was done. Small collections of photographs have been issued in Moscow and they merely skim the surface of the pictorial archive that comprises millions of negatives and prints.

This having been said, there is no question that we have here the finest collection of photography to come out of the war on the Eastern Front. The selection of pictures was made by two Czech editors, Daniela Mrazkova and Vladimir Remes, and the book was first published in Prague. The work has not been published in the Soviet Union.

The sampling presented clearly justifies Soviet comparisons of the best of their war photography with the work of Robert Capa, Alfred Eisenstadt, David Seymour, Henri Cartier-Bresson and David Douglas Duncan.

Vast as was the scale of war on the Eastern Front, the skill and bravery of Soviet cameramen captured enough to convey to us a deep feeling of its bitter depths.

# I. Invasion

*The German invasion of Russia began without warning on June 22, 1941. The inhabitants of Moscow were taken by surprise, as was Stalin himself. Much of the Soviet Air Force was destroyed on the ground. The Germans took over half a million prisoners. By the end of July the German Army Group Center was at Smolensk. Their northern army was approaching Leningrad and their southern army was approaching Kiev. The Germans had expected the Soviet armies to disintegrate under such defeats as the French armies had done in the previous year. Instead the Soviet Front was still unbroken and new armies were coming into action.*

*The Germans halted for a month while they considered what to do next—a loss of precious time. On August 23 Hitler decided against a direct advance on Moscow and ordered instead an invasion of the Ukraine. Again there were great German victories: nearly a million prisoners taken, the Ukraine, the Donets Basin and most of the Crimea occupied. Soviet Russia would have lost all its industrial strength if much of it had not already* *been moved beyond the Urals. At the end of September the German advance on Moscow was resumed. Once more there were great German victories: eight Soviet armies were destroyed. Hitler announced: "The enemy is broken and will never be in a position to rise again."*

*In Moscow there was panic. Crowds besieged the railway stations and the trains bound for the east. Martial law was proclaimed and the political police opened fire. The Soviet government moved to Kuibyshev. But Stalin remained in Moscow. On November 6 he addressed the Moscow Soviet meeting in an underground railway station. On November 7 he took the salute at the traditional military parade, somewhat diminished, in the Red Square. On December 2 the Germans came within sight of Moscow. They could go no further. The German attack was broken off. On December 5 Zhukov ordered a general offensive on the Moscow Front. The Germans were driven back. Though they then held their positions until the thaw came, their hopes of a quick victory faded. The Blitzkrieg was over.*

Mikhail Trakhman recalls, "It was indeed a magic force which made all of us war correspondents do everything in our power to prove that we were as ready and willing to sacrifice our lives as the armed soldiers were."

Trakhman was on flying missions between the central command and partisan units in the Leningrad, Kalinin and Pskov regions. As the German front retreated, he advanced with partisans to Byelorussia, the Ukraine and Poland, working behind the lines 2–250 miles from the front.

Once the fascists realized that a Soviet photojournalist was working behind their lines, they knew that Trakhman had a better idea of the positions of their troops than some of their own commanders and set a price on his head. The partisan command, however, took good care of Trakhman: they assigned two bodyguards to him and had both his camera and boxes containing exposed film wrapped with grenades so that all confidential material could be easily destroyed in case of an emergency. Whenever they faced a dangerous situation, the elder of the two guards would say reassuringly, "Don't worry, Misha, we won't let them take you alive."

It's rather paradoxical that Trakhman's most brilliant photographs—dynamic and humanistic pictures that are brilliantly composed—were created under these dangerous conditions. The secret of Trakhman's success can be traced to the drama that the war itself staged before his camera; it was merely a question of waiting for the right moment and selecting the proper angle. Of all his war pictures, Trakhman's favorite is his simple portrait of the young partisan, Alexei Grinchuk. This picture was taken in June during the time of the midnight sun, some 130 miles from Leningrad. Partisans had cut off all supply routes used by the enemy to bring reinforcements to the front, which forced the Nazis to send several divisions against the partisan brigade. At 6:00 in the morning, after a long march, Grinchuk suddenly said to Trakhman, who was lying next to him at the edge of a birch grove, "Take a picture of me." This was such an unusual request that the reporter was entirely taken aback. The enemy was aiming at them and he was afraid to make a move. But Grinchuk insisted. And so Trakhman photographed the young man just as he was —lying there on the ground at dawn. In less than 20 minutes the fighting broke out again and they had to cross the plain. Grinchuk was covering the retreat but was wounded and could not catch up with the others. As the Nazis closed in on him and he realized there was no hope of rescue, he shouted *prostitye* ("excuse me") and pulled the pin of his hand grenade.

Trakhman's films are no longer marked NFP ("not for the press"), a label used to ensure that no confidential information would reach the enemy. Trakhman, however, still lives with the memories of war. He still remembers the order given by commanders when food was scarce to save rations for the press photographers since "they do not live for the present but record what is happening now for future generations."

Trakhman, who is now a reporter for *Literaturnaya Gazeta* (*Literary Gazette*), a member of the Soviet Writers' Union and the author of numerous photographic books, still finds it necessary to return to the subject of the war. "I don't feel that I have yet managed to come to grips with the war nor have I depicted it in all its horror," he writes. "This does not represent my admiration for war but for peace. It is my desire to create a textbook for young people so that they will not forget. . . ."

Ivan Shagin.
Moscow, June 22, 1941.

YEVGENI KHALDEI.
Moscow, June 22, 1941.
Ten Minutes After Noon.

IVAN SHAGIN.  In the Village of Yushkovo, Moscow Region, 1941.

MIKHAIL TRAKHMAN. Fall, 1941.

Max Alpert. Late Fall.

ANATOLI GARANIN. Air Raid, Ukraine.

ANATOLI GARANIN. Near the Northwestern Front.

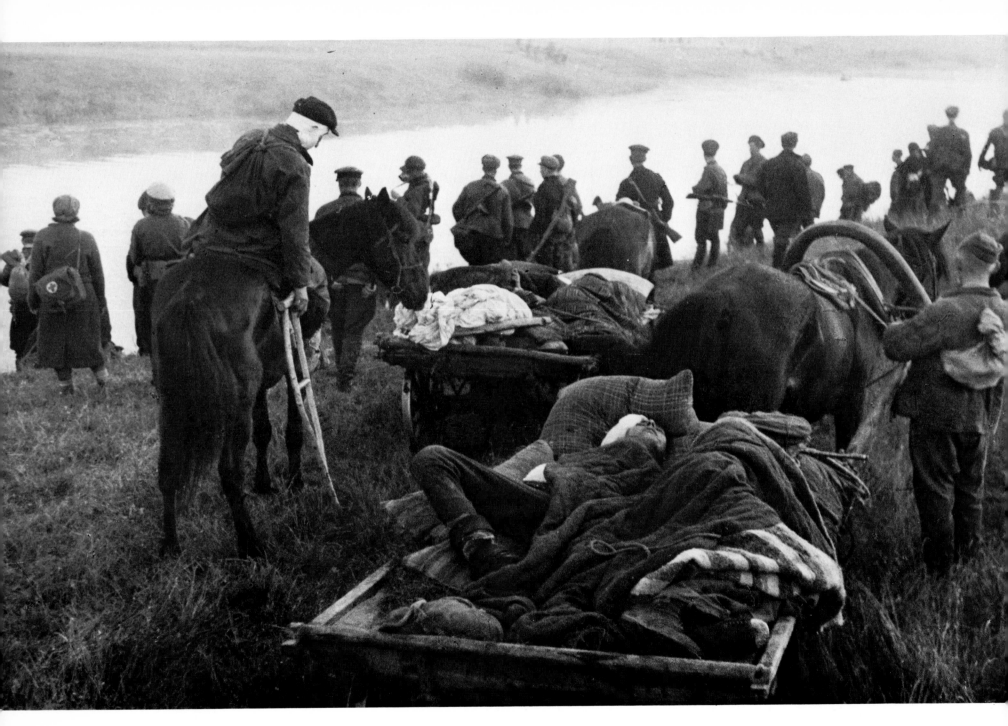

MIKHAIL TRAKHMAN. Falling Back.

GALINA SANKOVA. Yushkovo Village Farmers.

MIKHAIL TRAKHMAN. Evacuation. (*series of 3 pictures*)

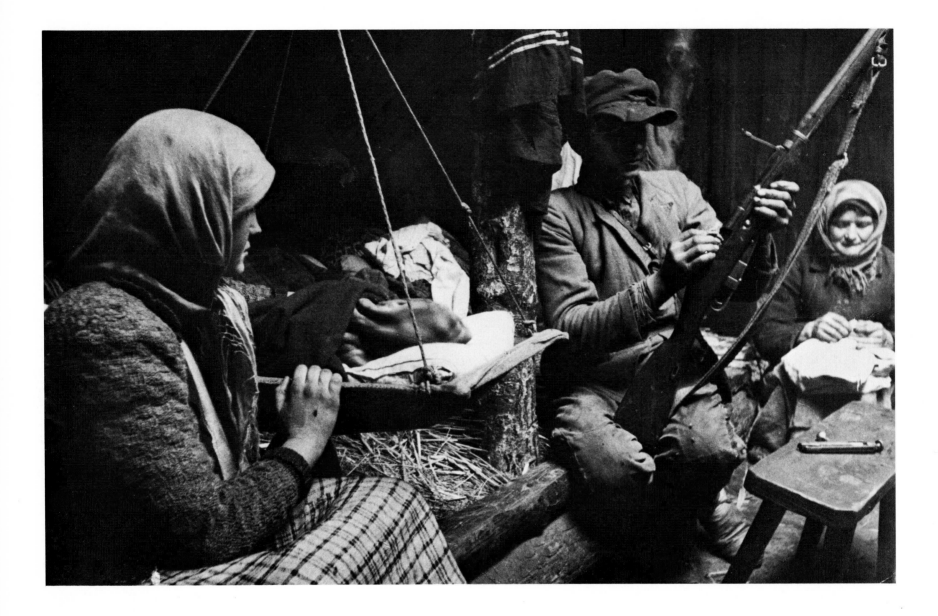

MIKHAIL TRAKHMAN. A Byelorussian Partisan.

MIKHAIL TRAKHMAN. Field Hospital.

MIKHAIL TRAKHMAN. Bread for the Partisans.

Mikhail Trakhman. The Partisans Attack. (*series of 4 pictures*)

DMITRI BALTERMANTS.

ALEXANDER USTINOV. MOSCOW.

ALEXANDER USTINOV. Muscovites Digging Trenches to Stop the Tanks.

DMITRI BALTERMANTS. Moscow, November 7, 1941.

ALEXANDER USTINOV. Fighting Outside Moscow. (*series of 2 pictures*)

ARKADI SHAYKHET. German Prisoners of War, Early Winter, 1941.

Ivan Shagin. 40-Degree-Below-Zero Weather, Moscow, December, 1941.

ANATOLI GARANIN. A Breach in the Blockade, Volkhov Front, 1941.

GALINA SANKOVA.
Ill-Equipped for Russian Soil,
December, 1941.

# II. Leningrad

*Leningrad fought a war all its own. German armies reached the suburbs of Leningrad at the beginning of September, 1941. German tanks attempted to force their way into the city streets. After a month's fighting they were stopped and never tried to break in again. But Leningrad was almost completely surrounded and was kept going only by supplies brought on railway tracks laid across Ladoga Lake when it froze. The siege of Leningrad continued until January, 1944. Out of the three million inhabitants over a million died of starvation and hardship. Yet life went on. Schools remained open except in the coldest weather. Factories still kept working hours. Leningrad sustained its name as the Hero City.*

Boris Kudoyarov photographed Leningrad under extraordinary circumstances that can be imagined today only with great difficulty. As people struggled to live amidst ruins, exploding bombs and artillery fire and were daily exposed to cold and starvation, events took on unprecedented significance. At a time when death was more common than a slice of bread and the sight of a dead person being dragged uncovered on a sled was more ordinary than that of a moving tram, all that was not totally essential was eliminated. Everything that had been commonplace before the war—food cooking on a warm stove, a burning lamp, even an open window—suddenly assumed a new meaning; they became synonymous with happiness and freedom.

The blockade of Leningrad lasted for 900 long, terrible days. For 900 days Boris Kudoyarov, the photographer/reporter for *Komsomolskaya Pravda,* lived and suffered and fought with the inhabitants of that city. He photographed the fighting near the besieged town and everyday life in the streets, factories, schools and homes. His pictorial poem of the besieged city includes 3,000 pictures that rank, in human and artistic value, on a par with the best works of art inspired by the heroic resistance of Leningrad.

Boris Kudoyarov was sent to the Leningrad front from Moscow on the first day war was declared. Because air transport had been disrupted, he went by train across Vologda, detouring around Ladoga Lake. He found the city on alert awaiting the advancing enemy.

The year 1941 was the worst. Millions of people retreating from the Baltic area had poured into Leningrad. The enemy sealed off the crowded city in such a way that the only possible supply route for food and ammunition was via Ladoga Lake. The route across the lake was called *doroga zhizni,* or "the road of life." In summer it went across the water, in winter across the ice. Daily bread rations dropped to a little over 3 ounces per person.

Leningrad became a front-line city. The fascists were halted at the city's borders. Every day at 2:00 P.M., when the people were leaving the factories, the German artillery went into action. And yet the people preserved at least the appearance of a normal daily life. When a school had been raided during the night, lessons often continued the following day on the stairs of the damaged building or in front of the school. And even though the workers had to face artillery fire at the factory gates, every effort was made to conform to regular working hours.

Other well-known reporters who photographed Leningrad during the siege included Anatoli Garanin, Galina Sankova, Alexander Ustinov and others. Yet these reporters merely visited Leningrad, recognizing it as an unusually dangerous sector of the front. Their experience of the disaster could therefore never equal that of Boris Kudoyarov, who hardly left the city during those three terrible years. Kudoyarov spent a brief time photographing the Baltic Fleet, and twice he visited the Hango Peninsula in the Baltic Sea.

Kudoyarov's pictorial testimony to the heroic defense of Leningrad, of the suffering of families, women and children, is an unparalleled photographic epic.

ANATOLI GARANIN. Leningrad Front, Winter, 1941–1942.

Mikhail Savin. Outside Vitebsk, Winter, 1941–1942.

Boris Kudoyarov. Pukovo Region, December, 1941.

BORIS KUDOYAROV. The Barricade at Gatchina.

BORIS KUDOYAROV. Nievsky Prospect.

Boris Kudoyarov. Air Raid, Leningrad. (*series of 2 pictures*)

BORIS KUDOYAROV.
Finding Water.

BORIS KUDOYAROV.
1,300,000 Died During
the 900-Day Siege
of Leningrad.

Boris Kudoyarov. Volkovo Cemetery.

MIKHAIL TRAKHMAN.
Life Goes On.

# III. Grief

*In the Crimea—where Sebastopol was already besieged—a landing was made on the peninsula of Kerch in the spring of 1942 to relieve the besieged city. In May the Germans struck back. Kerch had to be evacuated with the loss of 176,000 men and 350 tanks.*

Dmitri Baltermants worked as a war correspondent throughout the entire war. He took dozens of pictures daily, providing readers with pictorial reportage of current events. This probably explains why he, like Robert Capa, who first achieved fame for his photograph of the Spanish Civil War, has a definite attitude toward war. "War is, above all, grief. I photographed it nonstop for years, and I know that in all that time I produced only five or six real photographs. War is not for photography."

It is in the conflict between factual reporting and artistic transfiguration that we can trace the significance of Baltermants's work. The criteria used in evaluating photography have changed considerably with the passage of time. Much of what was considered first-class photography 30 years ago is now deemed mere documentation, while some photographs that would never have been published during the war because they were not considered relevant in a journalistic sense are now being rediscovered and admired for their artistic value. Dmitri Baltermants admits today: "If, heaven forbid, I had to photograph war again, I would do it quite differently. I agonize now at the thought of all of the things that I did not photograph."

"I was in Kerch, a seaport in the Crimea, together with Baltermants in the spring of 1942," writes author Konstantin Simonov. "Several pages of my diary are filled with notes describing that event. And yet this photograph reveals something of which I was not aware, that I did not notice or even think about. It is this unknown 'something' that separates art photography from ordinary photography."

Dmitri Baltermants's photographs reveal dramatically the naked emotion of human suffering. Baltermants was the war correspondent for *Izvestiya* and various army newspapers. He was moving on to another section of the front to photograph military operations when he was halted at Kerch. The events in Kerch were just one of a series of the countless, emotionally stirring scenes he witnessed.

A photographer can achieve sudden fame with one

picture; it can also happen that one photograph can penetrate the reality of inhuman acts better than words. One of Dmitri Baltermants's photographs played such a role. In 1965 he sent one picture entitled "Grief" (page 62) from his Kerch series to the world exhibition in Hamburg, "What Is Man?" During the five years of this traveling exhibition, the prize-winning picture was seen by people in almost every country in the world. The picture, "Grief," led to fame for Baltermants. *Life, Stern,* *Paris Match*—all the major photographic magazines—requested permission to publish it. Large headlines appeared in the Italian press hailing Baltermants as the "Soviet Robert Capa," comparing him favorably to the late American war photographer.

Baltermants's journalistic experience, his ability to react immediately, his feel for the dramatic development of an event—all of these qualities have made him a first-rate photojournalist.

MIKHAIL SAVIN.  Cavalry and Infantry Attack at Smolensk, September, 1942.  (*series of 2 pictures*)

ANATOLI GARANIN. Kerch, A Seaport in the Crimea, Spring, 1942. (*series of 2 pictures*)

DMITRI BALTERMANTS.

IVAN SHAGIN. Political Commissar Directing the Fighting.

DMITRI BALTERMANTS. Tanks Attack. (*series of 2 pictures*)

YAKOV RYUMKIN.

MIKHAIL TRAKHMAN.
A Pause in the Fighting.

ANATOLI GARANIN. Briansk Front, Summer, 1941—Crime and Punishment. (*series of 2 pictures*)

DMITRI BALTERMANTS.  Searching for Loved Ones at Kerch. (*series of 2 pictures*)

DMITRI BALTERMANTS. Grief.
(*series of 2 pictures*)

ALEXANDER UZLYAN.  The Black Sea Marines, Captured in This Dramatic Series
by Uzlyan in 1942, Were Known as "Black Death" by the Nazis. (*series of 5 pictures*)

# IV. Stalingrad

*The German advance on Stalingrad began on June 28. A month later Hitler rang up his Army Chief of Staff, Halder, and said, "The Russian is finished." Halder replied, "I must admit, it looks like it." The Russians had now learned how to retreat. There were no fresh encirclements. The Russian armies survived, though weakened. On August 23 the Germans under Paulus reached the Volga. Stalingrad straggled for some twenty miles along the river's banks. Hence it could not be encircled. It had to be taken by assault. Fierce combats went on for three months. The Russians contested every house and factory. German strength was gradually worn down. Soviet reinforcements increased.*

*The left flank of the Germans was covered by the River Don and guarded only by the armies of their allies, the Romanians and the Hungarians. The German generals believed that the Russians were incapable of a new offensive. They were wrong. On September 19 Stalin agreed on Zhukov's proposal to take the Germans in the rear. Few reinforcements were sent to Stalingrad. The bulk went far away behind the German lines.*

*On November 19 six Russian armies broke through the Romanian and German lines north and south of Stalingrad. On November 23 the two attacking forces met near Kalach. It was now Paulus's turn to be encircled. Hitler forbade any withdrawal and Paulus obeyed. Attempts were made to relieve the encircled armies. They failed. On January 31, 1943, Paulus, who had just been made a field marshal, surrendered. A quarter of a million German soldiers were lost. Ninety-one thousand went into captivity from which only 6,000 returned. It was the turn of the tide.*

Stalingrad was the third Soviet city where the front stopped. Retreat beyond the Volga was impossible. The heroic city transformed its ruins into a fortress that withstood the German onslaught. The Soviet armies marched from the "Stalingrad Basin," where the enemy was completely subdued, directly to the German border. Whenever Stalingrad and its defenders are discussed, the photographs of Georgi Zelma, a reporter for *Izvestiya* at the time, come immediately to mind. Zelma's pictorial essay of Stalingrad may be compared to Kudoyarov's pictures of besieged Leningrad.

When war broke, Zelma was on a business trip in

Kishinev. The editors of *Izvestiya* immediately sent him to Odessa, where he photographed preparations for the defense of that city. The defense, however, did not withstand the attack. During the evacuation, *Izvestiya* sent Zelma from the southernmost defense position of the 600-mile-long front to the northernmost position—the Rybachi and Sredni peninsulas. It was there that Zelma met the writer, Konstantin Simonov, and they recorded the defense of the country's northern frontiers. During 1941 Zelma was sent to Leningrad. He photographed near Tikhvin and later visited the Voronezh front. He also took part in the winter offensive at Kharkov, where he stayed until the spring of 1942, surviving a defeat during which many war reporters were killed in action with the troops. From there he went directly to Stalingrad.

Zelma arrived in Stalingrad before it had become a front-line city and stayed for four months—from the first day of fighting to the last. He experienced the bitterest moments of the struggle as well as the joy of victory and attempted to capture the spirit of the battle in his pictures. The struggle of man against man and the fight for every room of every house are reflected in his tension-filled combat photographs.

When, after the victory at Stalingrad, the front moved westward, Georgi Zelma returned to liberated Odessa after an absence of three years. He was therefore able to complement the pictures he had taken at the beginning of the war recording the tragedy and sorrow of the retreat with pictures illustrating the joys of victory.

In contrast to other photographers, who represented newspapers and wire services at the front for various periods of time, Georgi Lipskerov lived there. He was in the front lines throughout the war as a photographer and editor of an army newspaper in Stalingrad. Since he was so involved with the duties of his own regiment, Lipskerov was not free to go to other battlegrounds and envied his more peripatetic colleagues from the larger newspapers and agencies. Yet it was Lipskerov's unit that smashed the Sixth Army Corps of Field Marshal Paulus near Stalingrad. And it was Captain Lipskerov who was one of the first to photograph this great victory, including poignant pictures of the Field Marshal and his staff as they were led away as prisoners of war. Lipskerov was wearing the uniform of an ordinary soldier at the time, and Paulus, thinking that an elderly soldier was taking a snapshot as a souvenir, did not even attempt to strike the haughty pose he assumed a few moments later when faced with correspondents whom he immediately recognized as journalists.

Lipskerov was with the soldiers during the toughest battles; he carried his Leica on his chest like a weapon, ready to shoot at any moment. No wonder that, even in the most bitter cold, he would place his camera near the stove before sitting down to warm himself in order to prevent any damage to the sensitive instrument.

Lipskerov's passion for the camera is perhaps best illustrated by one incident. One day he came across a young German soldier among the trenches in the forest. Although it was a matter of life and death, Lipskerov pressed the shutter of his camera rather than the trigger of his gun. The result was a photograph depicting the amazement of a young man who, expecting immediate death, was captured on film instead.

Georgi Zelma. Stalingrad in February, 1943.

YAKOV RYUMKIN. Reinforcements Entering Stalingrad, September, 1942.

YAKOV RYUMKIN. Fighting in the Workshops of the Red October Plant.

GEORGI ZELMA.
Streetfighting in Stalingrad Where
Hitler Sacrificed 600,000 Germans.

GEORGI ZELMA. Fighting for Every Floor, November, 1942.

GEORGI ZELMA.
Fighting in the Suburbs of
Stalingrad, August, 1942.

GEORGI ZELMA. Fighting in the Suburbs of Stalingrad, November, 1942.

GEORGI ZELMA.
December, 1942.

GEORGI LIPSKEROV. House-to-House Fighting, December, 1942. (*series of 2 pictures*)

YAKOV RYUMKIN.

GEORGI LIPSKEROV.
Field Marshal Paulus Is Taken
Prisoner of War at Beketovka near
Stalingrad in February, 1943.

GEORGI ZELMA. First Bread for the Prisoners, February, 1943.

GEORGI ZELMA.   A Mass Grave of Soviet Defenders, Stalingrad, January, 1943.

# V.  West on the Trail of Horror

*After the victory of Stalingrad, Soviet armies began an advance that was to carry them into Germany and central Europe. They fought two great battles: at Kursk in July, 1943, when the German Army was for the first time decisively beaten in the field, and against the German Army Group Center in June, 1944, when the Germans lost 28 divisions and 350,000 German prisoners were taken. After each victory the Russians switched to another front and kept their advance moving steadily forward.*

*Each of the two years had its own character. 1943 was the year of liberation when Soviet soil was cleared of the enemy. There were rejoicings and family reunions. 1944 was the year of conquest when the Soviet armies reached German soil. Romania surrendered. Hungary was entered and by January, 1945, Soviet forces were in Austria.*

There were only five women with cameras who photographed the war: Natasha Bode, Olga Ignatovich, Olga Lander, Yelzaveta Mikulina and Galina Sankova. Of the five, Galina Sankova is the best known, and rightfully so. She has been an active photographer since the 1930s, and her work as a reporter has taken her to Siberia and to the construction sites of the Five- and Seven-Year plans as well as to the front lines during World War II.

Unlike other women reporters who photographed the war, Galina Sankova was not a war correspondent when the war started. She was first trained as a nurse, then as a driver and mechanic, but was not sent to the front until she became a correspondent for the magazine, *Frontovaya Illyustracia* (*The Front Illustrated*).

After one battle, she tended about 100 wounded men and was twice wounded seriously herself. The second of these injuries occurred during an airplane flight from Moscow to Petrozavodsk when something went wrong with the aircraft's fuel supply. Although the steering gear was not affected, a forced landing seemed out of the question because of boulders and trees on the ground below. The airplane landed and flipped over. After the accident Sankova was hospitalized with serious injuries. Despite doctor's orders she left the hospital the next day and managed to make it to Petrozavodsk.

In Petrozavodsk she took her famous picture of the children's concentration camp. Several years ago she tracked down one of the girls who was in that picture and photographed her again as a student at the university. The two portraits won her a gold medal at the Interpressphoto Exhibit in Moscow.

"Difficulties don't exist for me and I don't care about bad food or discomfort. I try to overcome all this the same way that men do. And that's how it was at the front," says Galina Sankova. Yet she will never forget the terrible time at the Leningrad front. There was nothing but ruins and destruction, nowhere to sleep or get warm. When asked if her male colleagues helped her, Sankova replied: "I always had to look after myself, as they had enough to do worrying about themselves."

Was she ever afraid? Of course. Many times she even wished for death when bullets whistled around her. Yet she had a mission, and, despite orders to the contrary, she always managed to get sent into battle with a fighting unit. "Maybe there is something feminine in my pictures because, after all, I am a woman," she admits, "but I really don't know what it would be, as I've been living like a man too long."

Galina Sankova considers all of her war pictures a coherent whole, which she's entitled "On the Trail of Horror"—horror left behind by the Germans. Her pictures take us back to the cruelty of the slaughter of civilians with no mercy shown toward children, to the time when cultural treasures and monuments were wantonly destroyed. "I wanted to show future generations all that horror in my photographs," says Sankova.

Max Alpert's photographs are a chronicle of the Soviet state in pictures. As a reporter for the press, he photographed the difficult period after the Civil War; Maxim Gorky's return from Italy; the rescue of the expedition led by General Nobile; construction of the first Five-Year plans; and the battles of the Red Army during World War II.

"My ideas on how to photograph the war were naive," admits Max Alpert. "The first time I was under fire I was unable to take a single picture. I didn't know where to turn or where to look first. When the battle was over, I noticed a striking sight: helmets, lost rifles and discarded ammunition strewn about the trodden ground. I told myself that when I calmed down I would take a picture of that still life. But then everything went black again and there was another volley of fire between us and the enemy. I jumped into a trench where I saw a number of small, gray mice running around. I'm ashamed to admit it but, in spite of the shots being fired all around me, I jumped out of the trench and sought refuge in a nearby crater. Of course, I never took a picture of that still life. It had disappeared. And I realized that one cannot plan ahead in wartime—men and things exist only for the moment."

As a result of this experience, Alpert took a picture that brought him fame. The picture, which was a portrait of Battalion Commander A. G. Yeryomenko, the combat commander of Alpert's regiment—his hand spread out as if ready to dance while holding his pistol firmly at the same time—elicited countless inquiries concerning the identity of the soldier when it first appeared in the Soviet press. The whole nation seemed to identify with the portrait and it became a symbol of the victorious advance of the Soviet Army west into Europe.

GALINA SANKOVA.
Spring in the Ukraine, 1943.

GALINA SANKOVA. Returning Home, 1943.

GALINA SANKOVA. Russian Children in a Concentration Camp at Petrozavodsky.

IVAN SHAGIN. On the Road, 1943.

MIKHAIL SAVIN. German Cemetery near Smolensk.

Mikhail Savin. Homecoming, Ulyanovo, July, 1943.

Mark Redkin. The Enemy Has Gone, Smolensk, Fall, 1944.

ANATOLI GARANIN. Brief Reunion, 1942.

IVAN SHAGIN. Among the Ruins, Orlovsk Region, 1943.

MARK REDKIN. Home Leave, 1943. (*series of 2 pictures*)

MARK REDKIN.
Mother and Son, 1943.

ARKADI SHAYKHET. Our Brother and Son, 1944.

Max Alpert. The Regimental Commander, 1942.

MAX ALPERT. Tank Attack, 1944.

EMMANUJEL YEVZERIKHIN.
Artillery, 1944.

GEORGI ZELMA. Reconnaissance.

MIKHAIL SAVIN. Tanks in Action, 1943.

MAX ALPERT. Partisans, 1944.

MAX ALPERT. Getting Across, 1944.

MIKHAIL TRAKHMAN. Near Miss.

IVAN SHAGIN. Direct Hit.

DMITRI BALTERMANTS. Moving Across the Oder, 1944.

RAFAIL DIAMENT. North Sea Navy, 1944.

YEVGENI KHALDEI. Into Austria, April, 1945.

MIKHAIL SAVIN.
Konigsberg, April, 1945.

ARKADI SHAYKHET.
They, Too, Experienced Sorrow,
Konigsberg, 1945.

ALEXANDER USTINOV.
Poland, 1945.

# VI.  On to Berlin

*The Germans did not take Moscow. The Russians took Berlin. This was their last and, as they felt, their crowning achievement of the war. The Russian advance began on April 16 with two million men and 6,300 tanks. On April 30, Hitler killed himself and his wife Eva Braun whom he had married the previous day. The commander of the Berlin garrison surrendered on May 2. There was no formal capitulation. The Russians simply took over the city and ran it until the Allied contingents arrived to share the task.*

*Berlin had lost all military significance except as a center of communications. Its capture was merely symbolic as the end of the Reich, and the supreme symbol was the Reichstag, an empty shell since the fire there in February 1933.*

When the attack on Berlin began in April of 1945 Viktor Tyomin, a special correspondent for *Pravda,* devised a plan to get the first picture of the victorious Soviet flag atop Berlin's Reichstag for his paper. He and his colleague, the movie cameraman, Roman Karmen, had three tanks and one airplane at their disposal. The plan was that as the tanks neared their destination in Berlin, the crews would signal Veshtak, the pilot of the aircraft, via radio who would then pick up Tyomin and Karmen at a field airport where they stood ready.

The long-awaited moment came on the first of May. When Veshtak took off with Tyomin (due to illness, Karmen did not accompany them), he had no idea of the purpose behind the mission. If he had known he probably never would have left the ground, as they were surrounded by fighting on all sides and were in constant danger. The plane was hit several times but Tyomin never stopped photographing. At the very moment when they passed over the Reichstag and Tyomin pressed the shutter of his camera, he realized that he had just used his last exposure.

The real difficulty still lay ahead: how to get the valuable document to *Pravda*'s editorial offices in Moscow, thousands of miles away. Wirephoto teletype did not exist at that time and Veshtak refused to fly the damaged plane on to Moscow. Tyomin refused to give up. He telephoned Marshal Zhukov, chief commander of the front, who agreed to lend Tyomin his own plane—on the condition that it would be flown only as far as the Polish town of Januv. But that wasn't good enough if the photographs were to reach the news desk in time to make the following day's edition of the paper in which the Army Victory Order would appear. Assuming all responsibility, Tyomin ordered the pilot to fly on to Moscow. They managed to safely bypass anti-aircraft fire on the border and the fighter planes near Leningrad. By 2:00 A.M. Tyomin was able to deliver his pictures to the office in Moscow.

Even before the new edition of the paper had gone to press, Tyomin learned that Marshal Zhukov had issued orders that Tyomin was to be shot for stealing the plane. There was even some suspicion that Tyomin was a fraud and had never really reached Berlin. At 7:00 A.M. on August 3, Tyomin returned to Berlin with 20,000 copies of *Pravda* just off the press. At 2:00 P.M. on the same day, he distributed the papers in front of the Reichstag to his astonished colleagues. "A group of more than sixty correspondents would have liked to have torn me to pieces on the spot, and I'm sure that even today, thirty years later, some of them have not forgiven me for what I did," Tyomin recalls with a smile.

The next day Tyomin's picture was picked up by all the leading world newspapers. The BBC in London questioned whether the edition of *Pravda* featuring the photograph had somehow been printed in Berlin. The British *News Chronicle* wrote that ". . . this is one of the historic monuments of war that will live on, even in peacetime." Finally, Tyomin decided to confront Zhukov. Up to this time he could have been arrested at any moment since Zhukov's orders had not been rescinded. "You deserve a hero's medal for your action but for your lack of discipline in stealing the aircraft of a front commander, you deserve punishment. Therefore, you will only receive the Red Star Order," the Marshal decided.

IVAN SHAGIN. On to Berlin, 1945.

IVAN SHAGIN. From Himmler's House to the Reichstag, May 1, 1945.

IVAN SHAGIN. To the Center of Berlin. (*series of 2 pictures*)

YEVGENI KHALDEI.

VIKTOR TYOMIN.  Banner of Victory Flies over the Reichstag, May 1, 1945.

VIKTOR GREBNEV. On the Way to the Reichstag.

VIKTOR GREBNEV. Reichstag, as Seen from the Cellar of Himmler's House.

IVAN SHAGIN. Fighting for the Reichstag.

Yakov Ryumkin.  The Banner of Victory, Reichstag, May 1, 1945.

YEVGENI KHALDEI. Victory.

Yevgeni Khaldei. Victors' Signatures, Berlin, 1945.

Ivan Shagin.  May 2, 1945.

Ivan Shagin.
Prisoners at the
Brandenburg Gate.

VIKTOR GREBNEV.
The Stalingrad
to Berlin Dance.

DMITRI BALTERMANTS.
Music and Flowers.

MIKHAIL TRAKHMAN.
Let the Soldiers Sleep. (*series of 2 pictures*)

GEORGI LIPSKEROV.

MARK REDKIN.
The End.

# VII. Echoes

The war ended long ago but it still lives on in the memory of the people. Sometimes it serves as a warning to future generations, as in the message on the Memorial in the Byelorussian village of Khatin, which was razed by the Nazis on March 22, 1943:

PEOPLE, DEFEND LIFE, RID THE SUN OF THE LEADEN CLOUDS, THE BLUE SKY OF THE TERRIBLE SMOKE OF BURNING, THE LIFE-GIVING FIELD OF THE RAVAGING HANDS OF MOLOCH'S ARMIES. YOU MUST NEVER ALLOW ANYTHING LIKE THIS TO HAPPEN AGAIN.

Two press photographers from Minsk, Alexandra and Mikhail Ananin, are still photographing the aftermath of the war on the site of the Khatin tragedy. Their first photographs of the holocaust of war were not taken here, however, but at the Brest-Litovsk fortress, which they visited for the first time in 1961. As press photographers, they took part in a meeting of former defenders of this fortress who, because of their unyielding resistance, had even won the respect of the enemy. From that time on, Alexandra and Mikhail Ananin have been attending the Brest-Litovsk meetings regularly. Since they have come to know most of the defenders well, they are not regarded as mere reporters and have therefore succeeded in producing spontaneous, deeply emotional pictures that are an eloquent testimony to the suffering endured by the Byelorussian people.

Yevgeni Khaldei. May, 1945.

MAX ALPERT. Victory Day on Moscow's Red Square, May 9, 1945.

Yevgeni Khaldei. Ruins in Murmansk, 1942.

YEVGENI KHALDEI. Vienna, April, 1945.

ALEXANDRA AND MIKHAIL ANANIN. Brest-Litovsk Fortification, 1965.

ALEXANDRA AND MIKHAIL ANANIN. National Memorial at Khatin, 1969.

ALEXANDRA AND MIKHAIL ANANIN. Brest-Litovsk Fortification, 1973.

ALEXANDRA AND MIKHAIL ANANIN.
Bell at Khatin, 1969.

# Biographical Sketches of Photographers

MAX ALPERT (b. 1899). Max Alpert, one of the pioneers of Soviet photojournalism, published his first photographs in 1924 and, together with A. Shaykhet, G. Petrusov, S. Fridlyand and other photographers of his generation, was responsible for making journalistic photography the equal of other more traditional genres. During World War II he was a correspondent for TASS and photographed battles of the Fourth Ukrainian Front in Czechoslovakia. In 1959 he became a reporter for the Soviet Information Bureau and is now working for the Novosti News Agency.

MIKHAIL ANANIN (b. 1912), ALEXANDRA ANANIN (b. 1913). Mikhail Ananin, a Byelorussian photographer from Minsk, went to work for *Komsomolskaya Pravda* in 1931. When war broke out he was sent to the front as a press photographer and later fought with the partisan units. Twice seriously wounded, he was forced to undergo medical treatment after the war was over and still suffers as a result of his injuries. Alexandra began to collaborate with her husband after he was injured and together they were sent from Moscow to Minsk as correspondents for *Sovetsky Soyuz* (*Soviet Union*) magazine. They produced a number of picture essays about Byelorussia, but it is their photographs depicting war and its aftermath that have achieved the greatest popularity. Recently they have been joined by their daughter, Tamara, who is a reporter for *Sovetsky Soyuz*.

DMITRI BALTERMANTS (b. 1912). Dmitri Baltermants spent the entire war at the front as a correspondent for *Izvestiya* and the army newspaper, *Na Razgrom vraga* (*To Destroy the Enemy*). He photographed the defeat of the Germans near Moscow, the defense of Sevastopol, the Battle of Stalingrad, the liberation of southern USSR and battles in Poland.

Today Baltermants is chief press photographer for *Ogonyok* magazine, where he has worked for 30 years. He has also edited several photographic publications. Many of his photographic essays are well known, but most renowned are his pictures of war.

RAFAIL DIAMENT (b. 1907). After Diament's first photograph was published in 1927, he started working regularly for the press and, in 1937, moved to Moscow as a professional photojournalist. Throughout the war he served as a correspondent, reporting on the North Sea Fleet. He retired in 1969 but still publishes occasionally.

ANATOLI GARANIN (b. 1912). A photographer with a rich cultural background, Anatoli Garanin's photographic repertoire is not limited to journalism but also includes such genres as scenic and theater photography. During the war he was a reporter for *Frontovaya Illyustracia*. He now works as a special correspondent for *Sovetsky Soyuz* and is also affiliated with the Moscow theater, "Na Tagantse," where a permanent exhibition of his theatrical photographs is housed.

VIKTOR GREBNEV (b. 1907). Grebnev began photographing in the 1930s as a reporter. When war broke out, he joined the staff of the army newspaper, *Krasnaya zvezda* (*Red Star*), and was later transferred, at his own request, to the front-line newspaper, *Frontovik* (*The Front-line Fighter*). He was one of the photographers of the Soviet Banner of Victory that was hoisted over the Reichstag. After the war, Grebnev remained for several years in the Soviet zone of Germany as a press photographer. On his return to the USSR he became a sports reporter.

YEVGENI KHALDEI (b. 1916). As a reporter for *Pravda* and the TASS News Agency during World War II, Khaldei took part in the largest battles on Soviet soil. The last year of the war took him to Rumania, Bulgaria, Yugoslavia, Hungary, Austria and finally—like so many of his colleagues—to Berlin. He was one of the photographers at the Potsdam Conference and the trials at Nuremberg. His pictures of the war have been exhibited numerous times both at home and abroad. Khaldei is now on the staff of *Sovyetskaya Kultura* (*Soviet Culture*) magazine.

BORIS KUDOYAROV (1903–1973). One of the founders of Soviet photojournalism, Kudoyarov joined the ranks of the Red Army during the Civil War at the age of seventeen as platoon deputy commander. Before World War II, Kudoyarov worked for several magazines and news agencies; during the war he was a special correspondent for Moscow's *Komsomolskaya Pravda*. He was the only reporter to survive the 900-day blockade of Leningrad, and his photographic epic of Leningrad is a remarkable record of the battles as well as everyday life in the city. In 1973, Kudoyarov was killed in an automobile accident while photographing in Tashkent.

GEORGI LIPSKEROV (b. 1896). Lipskerov was one of the oldest photojournalists of World War II. He joined the staff of an army newspaper when he was almost fifty and spent the entire war at the front. His prior experience as an active sportsman was good preparation for life in the front lines. During the past few years he has been a photographer for various publications.

MARK REDKIN (b. 1908). Redkin's work for the army newspaper, *Krasnaya zvezda,* trained him as a war correspondent. During the war Redkin worked for TASS and *Frontovaya Illyustracia*. He photographed, among many other important events, the surrender of Germany. The war did not end in Berlin for Redkin. He visited liberated Prague and was later sent to the Japanese front. He now works for Planeta, a publishing house in Moscow.

YAKOV RYUMKIN (b. 1913). Ryumkin began to publish photographs in 1926. He worked for *Pravda* and *Ogonyok,* and is now with *Selskaya Nov* (*Agricultural News*) magazine. During the war he was a *Pravda* correspondent.

GALINA SANKOVA (b. 1904). Galina Sankova is the best known of the five women who were photojournalists during the war. Involved in photography since the thirties, she has succeeded in equaling the achievements of her male colleagues in spite of the many difficulties she encountered as a woman attempting to reach the front. She photographed the Western, Briansk and Don fronts near Stalingrad and the northern offensive of 1944 in besieged Leningrad for *Frontovaya Illyustracia*. Often laying aside her camera to serve as a nurse, Galina Sankova was twice seriously wounded herself. She is now on the staff of *Ogonyok* magazine.

MIKHAIL SAVIN (b. 1915). Mikhail Savin began his professional career in 1939 as a correspondent in Byelorussia for the TASS New Agency. During the war he was a reporter for the newspaper of the western part of the front, *Krasnoarmeyskaya Pravda* (*Red Army Pravda*). Since 1945 he has been in the photography department of *Ogonyok* magazine.

IVAN SHAGIN (b. 1904). Shagin's acquaintance with Roman Karmen, who was to become an outstanding photographer at the front, influenced him to become a photographer. Between 1932 and 1950, Shagin was the chief reporter for *Komsomolskaya Pravda*. Since 1950 he has worked for various Soviet publishing houses.

ARKADI SHAYKHET (1898–1959). Arkadi Shaykhet was one of the leaders of the group of Soviet photojournalists who came to the fore after the Revolution of 1917. He was one of the initiators of the movement in the twenties and thirties that elevated photographic reportage to the same level as literary reportage. His picture, "Thank You, Sons," ranks with Capa's "Fallen Fighter" and Baltermants's "Grief" as one of the most effective protests against the horrors of war ever photographed.

VIKTOR TYOMIN (b. 1908). Viktor Tyomin has been a reporter for various publications and has photographed in all parts of the USSR and in 28 foreign countries. He was the first to photograph the Soviet Banner of Victory over the Reichstag and was one of eight reporters in the world present at the execution of the major Nazi war criminals after the Nuremberg trial. In addition to being present at all fronts during World War II, he also took part in the fighting in Finland and was present at the surrenders of Germany and Japan. He is now correspondent for special assignments for the USRR Press Center.

MIKHAIL TRAKHMAN (b. 1918). When war broke out Trakhman was a special correspondent for TASS and later for the Soviet Information Bureau. He photographed not only at the various fronts but also behind the enemy lines. For the past 15 years he has been a special correspondent for the *Literaturnaya Gazeta,* but his main interest is the editing of pictorial books about World War II.

ALEXANDER USTINOV (b. 1909). Ustinov has spent half his life, including the war years, as a correspondent for *Pravda*. During the last two years of the war he was at the First Ukrainian Front, where he photographed the fighting by the First Czechoslovak Army Corps in the autumn of 1944 and the liberation of Czechoslovakia by the Red Army. He also photographed the meeting of Soviet and American forces on the Elbe near Berlin.

ALEXANDER UZLYAN (b. 1908). Alexander Uzlyan was a staff photographer for *Izvestiya, Pravda* and *Ogonyok* magazine. During World War II, he was assigned to the Black Sea Fleet (known as "Black Death" to the Germans) as a correspondent for the Soviet Information Bureau. He devoted a series of photographs to them as well as a book of memoirs, in which he attempted to express his great admiration for their feats. His photographs, which capture the bravery of the marines, give an impression of movement that is almost like a motion picture.

EMMANUEL YEVZERIKHIN (b. 1911). During World War II, Yevzerikhin was a photographer for TASS, but the aesthetic quality of his photographs was not appreciated until after peace had been declared. He is now a lecturer at the Peoples' University of Photography in Moscow and is also a free-lance reporter for TASS.

GEORGI ZELMA (b. 1906). In the twenties and thirties, Georgi Zelma was active in the development of modern Soviet photojournalism. He began photographing the war as a reporter for *Izvestiya* near Odessa, and later took part in the fighting on all fronts. His pictures of the Battle of Stalingrad merit special mention. When the war ended, Zelma was sent on many photographic assignments abroad and has published several pictorial books, including one devoted to the defense of Stalingrad.